THE
STONEWALL
RIOTS

THE FIGHT FOR LGBT RIGHTS

BY TRISTAN POEHLMANN

CONTENT CONSULTANT
CHRIS FREEMAN, PHD, PROFESSOR, ENGLISH AND
GENDER STUDIES, USC DORNSIFE COLLEGE OF
LETTERS, ARTS AND SCIENCES

Essential Library

An Imprint of Abdo Publishing | abdopublishing.com

ABDOPUBLISHING.COM

Published by Abdo Publishing, a division of ABDO, PO Box 398166, Minneapolis, Minnesota
55439. Copyright © 2017 by Abdo Consulting Group, Inc. International copyrights reserved in
all countries. No part of this book may be reproduced in any form without written permission
from the publisher. Essential Library™ is a trademark and logo of Abdo Publishing.

Printed in the United States of America, North Mankato, Minnesota
102016
012017

Cover Photo: Richard Corkery/New York Daily News/Getty Images
Interior Photos: Richard Drew/AP Images, 4–5; Bettmann/Getty Images, 7; Drew Angerer/
Getty Images News/Getty Images, 11; Red Line Editorial, 16–17, 52–53; iStockphoto, 18–19;
Mattachine Society of New York/From The New York Public Library, 23; Ed Ford/New York
World–Telegram and the Sun Newspaper Photograph Collection/Library of Congress, 25; Eddie
Adams/AP Images, 28; Chris O'Meara/AP Images, 30–31; Larry C. Morris/The New York
Times/Redux, 34; AP Images, 36, 70; New York Daily News Archive/Getty Images, 40–41;
Michelle V. Agins/The New York Times/Redux, 43; Photo by Diana Davies/Manuscripts and
Archives Division/The New York Public Library, 46, 67, 80, 84–85, 90; Jerry Engel/New York
Post Archives/© NYP Holdings, Inc./Getty Images, 54–55; Photo by Kay Tobin/©Manuscripts
and Archives Division/The New York Public Library, 58, 64–65, 74–75; Photo by Richard
Wandel courtesy LGBT Community Center National History Archive, 82; Eric Miller/AP
Images, 92; Dennis Van Tine/Sipa USA/AP Images, 95; Jason DeCrow/AP Images, 97

Editor: Heather C. Hudak
Series Designer: Maggie Villaume

PUBLISHER'S CATALOGING-IN-PUBLICATION DATA

Names: Poehlmann, Tristan, author.
Title: The Stonewall riots: the fight for LGBT rights / by Tristan Poehlmann.
Other titles: The fight for LGBT rights
Description: Minneapolis, MN : Abdo Publishing, 2017. | Series: Hidden heroes |
    Includes bibliographical references and index.
Identifiers: LCCN 2016945475 | ISBN 9781680783902 (lib. bdg.) |
    ISBN 9781680797435 (ebook)
Subjects: LCSH: Stonewall Riots, New York, N.Y., 1969--Juvenile literature. |
    Gay liberation movement--United States--History--20th century--Juvenile
    literature. | Gay rights--United States--History--Juvenile literature. | Gay men--
    United States--History--20th century--Juvenile literature. | Gays--United States-
    -History--20th century--Juvenile literature. | Greenwich Village (New York,
    N.Y.)--History--20th century--Juvenile literature.
Classification: DDC 306.76--dc23
LC record available at http://lccn.loc.gov/2016945475

CONTENTS

CHAPTER ONE
THE RIOT

On the humid night of June 27, 1969, people gathered at the back of a dark and dirty bar. They came every night—young gay men, transgender women, street youth, lesbians, and gender-nonconforming people. After long days of working on an assembly line, answering phones, or hustling on the avenues of New York City's Greenwich Village, they came to the Stonewall Inn for friendship and a drink.

In the corner, the jukebox churned, racking up dimes and pumping out anthems of love and heartache. By midnight, as June 28 began, nearly 200 regular patrons moved to the beat, the air thick and sticky on their skin. Here in the back room of a grimy bar, they felt strong and beautiful, showing off for

The Stonewall Inn is located at 53 Christopher Street in New York City.

one another and holding each other close. The bar was not a nice place. The glasses were never washed, and the windows were boarded up. But no one really cared about that. The bar was a place where they could feel loved and free from judgment.

Outside, a full moon hung high over New York City, witnessing the heat of the late June night. It was a night for endings and beginnings, for sparks and flames, for defiance and change. And in a room just a few blocks away, another group gathered.

The Vice Squad Takes Aim

Deputy Inspector Seymour Pine had a plan he had been working on for weeks. His unit, Manhattan's First Division of the Public Morals, was responsible for investigating organized crime, financial corruption, pornography, and prostitution. Often these cases involved the Mafia,

GREENWICH VILLAGE

Greenwich Village—often called simply "the Village"—is a neighborhood in lower Manhattan with a long history of radical politics. Since the first wave of bohemians moved there in the 1910s, alternative thinkers, artists, and lesbian, gay, bisexual, and transgender (LGBT) people have been at the center of its culture and community. In the 1950s, beatnik writers such as Allen Ginsberg called the Village home, writing books that shocked mainstream America. In the 1960s, artists such as Andy Warhol walked the streets of Greenwich Village alongside future leaders of the gay rights movement.

Beatniks were part of the beat movement. They wrote about their thoughts and feelings in a free, unstructured style.

and the Mafia often used gay bars as fronts for its illegal business dealings.

Pine had recently been assigned to a case involving international bonds theft, a serious financial crime. The New York Police Department traced the center of this operation to a particular Mafia-run gay bar in Pine's district. Now his unit gathered, ready to act. It was time to take down the Stonewall Inn.

Pine's plan was twofold, and the first part had gone off without a hitch. On Tuesday night, June 24, he and his officers had raided the Stonewall, confiscating liquor and gathering evidence to support a larger raid. Pine told the owner the bar was improperly licensed—it was registered as a private bottle club. Bottle clubs did not sell alcohol. They simply served members' personal bottles of alcohol in a social club setting. Pretending to be a bottle club was a common Mafia strategy to avoid the liquor laws that applied to public bars.

With that law violation, Pine was able to get a warrant to return for another raid on Friday night. This one would destroy the bar for the foreseeable future. He would once again confiscate any alcohol on the premises and arrest the Mafia employees. Then he would

THE MAFIA MONOPOLY ON GAY BARS

"Fat Tony" Lauria, the owner of the Stonewall Inn, was typical of most gay bar owners in 1960s New York. He was straight, involved with the Mafia, and interested in making lots of money. For years, the Mafia cornered the market on gay bars because of a loophole in the state's liquor laws. Until 1967, the law was vague on whether it was legal to serve alcohol to LGBT patrons. Most bars interpreted this as a ban and did not serve LGBT patrons. But the loophole appealed to the Mafia, which was willing to bribe police to ignore potential infractions. The profits from running a gay bar were often huge because there were few other places for LGBT people to gather.

seize the vending equipment, cut up the bar with a saw, and haul it all away. He would leave the Stonewall Inn bare and empty.

As his unit gathered at First Division headquarters, Pine reviewed the plan. He instructed several undercover officers, two of them women, to enter the bar before the raid. Their job was to watch the Mafia employees, find out who handled which job, and make notes for use in court. Then when Pine and his uniformed officers came through the door, the undercover officers would arrest the employees.

Based on his experience, Pine was certain no one would fight back. Patrons at Mafia-run gay bars were used to police raids and most were quick to run away. Police often arrested patrons during raids—typically people who caused trouble or lacked identification. When gay bar patrons were arrested, their names were printed in the newspaper and their lives were ruined by the public exposure. Afraid of being outed as gay, patrons ran as soon as they could, disappearing into the shadows. There was no reason why tonight's raid should go any differently.

In the Early Hours of the Morning

Inside the Stonewall Inn, someone slid another dime into the jukebox. The Rolling Stones' "I Can't Get No Satisfaction" wailed through the bar. Couples moved together in the spotlights, the beams casting their bodies into darkness and light. They twirled and shimmied, dancing and laughing. Others stood at the edge of the dance floor in the half-light, talking and drinking.

Suddenly, the bar lights shot up to full brightness. Music and chatter broke off. People squinted and turned, craning their necks to figure out what happened. Was it the cops? Police often stopped by to collect bribe money in exchange for not raiding the bar, but they usually left quickly. And there had already been a raid on Tuesday.

> "The best metaphors for Stonewall are words like *home*, because when you're not living anywhere regularly, home becomes what you make it."[1]
>
> –Stonewall patron and gay street youth Tommy Lanigan-Schmidt

Would the music come back on? Could they keep dancing?

Maria Ritter, a young transgender woman, saw cops heading for the dance floor. They grabbed and pushed people along. Scared of being caught, Ritter turned and ran toward the bathroom, hoping for a window to escape through. She did not even make it that far. An officer caught her arm and shoved her toward the back of the bar.

The police liked to separate patrons: women to one side, men to another, and gender-nonconforming

A sign inside the entrance of the Stonewall Inn reminds patrons of the events that took place there in June 1969.

people to the back near the bathrooms. It was a common scare tactic aimed at cross-dressing patrons. Officers threatened to examine their clothing and bodies if they would not confess to the crime of cross-dressing. If they resisted, women officers took them into the bathroom for a strip search. It was a humiliating ritual. But tonight, the patrons of

"My biggest fear was that I would get arrested. My second biggest fear is that my picture would be in a newspaper or on a television report in my mother's dress!"[2]

–Stonewall patron Maria Ritter

the Stonewall Inn were angry and not taking any flack. They yelled and fought, pushing back at the police.

Near the front of the bar, officers performing frisks touched several lesbians in inappropriate ways. The lesbians began to shout at the officers, alerting other patrons to the situation. The muttering rose to a boil as officers harassed the patrons, trying to control the room. As Deputy Inspector Pine kept an eye on the alcohol confiscation, he slowly realized matters were getting out of hand.

Finally, Pine allowed any men and women with identification to exit the bar. Gender-nonconforming people and people without identification had to remain inside. At the door, an officer checked each person's identification to make sure they were of legal drinking age. If not, they would be arrested. Slowly, the line inched

ANTI-CROSS-DRESSING LAWS

How many pieces of gender-conforming clothing must a person wear in order to avoid arrest? According to the laws of New York in the 1960s, the magic number was three. In practice, this meant that when police suspected a person of cross-dressing, they would examine that person's clothing—including underwear. This process was often humiliating and abusive. If the officer concluded that, for example, a butch lesbian was not wearing at least three items of women's clothing, she could be arrested. Such laws essentially criminalized expressions of gender nonconformity.

forward. As the patrons emerged into the hot night air, a strange and different mood spread through the group. Instead of running, they gathered together.

Across Christopher Street, a small triangular park sat opposite the Stonewall Inn. It was the perfect place for a crowd of spectators to watch events unfold. The exiting patrons started to play up the scene, posing dramatically as the crowd cheered and clapped. It was as if the Stonewall Inn doorway led to a runway or a stage. Each person upped the ante, flirting, dancing, or cracking jokes in resistance to the situation.

These subversive antics lasted until a police wagon pulled up, signaling arrests were about to begin. The crowd murmured worriedly. There were still many people inside the Stonewall Inn, including the gender-nonconforming patrons. Would they all be arrested?

After a long, tense moment, officers emerged from the bar with a small group of handcuffed transgender women. As the police roughly loaded the women into the police wagon, the crowd began to protest, yelling and throwing pennies at the cops—dirty coppers for dirty cops.

One transgender woman hit a cop with her purse in retaliation for him shoving her. The cop struck her with his nightstick. Boos filled the air, and hands smacked at the wagon. Then a butch lesbian was wrestled out of the bar in handcuffs, fighting all the way. A cop hit her on the head with his nightstick and tried to shove her into a squad car. She escaped, kicking and yelling, but the police dragged her back. Again she fought her way out, shouting at the crowd, "Why don't you guys do something?"[3]

The crowd broke. People pelted the police with spare change, nickels, and quarters. They heaved empty bottles and beer cans. They screamed and yelled until the police began panicking, unable to control the situation. Trapped between the bar and the angry crowd,

Deputy Inspector Pine made a decision. He and his officers retreated into the Stonewall Inn, barricaded the doors, and prepared for a siege. Outside, the riot boiled over.

Hidden Heroes

Inside and outside the Stonewall Inn, hundreds of brave people fought for themselves and for their community. Some of these people went on to become prominent activists. But many of them disappeared from historical memory or never received recognition for their acts.

The raid at the Stonewall Inn was a moment when many people stood up for the rights of lesbian, gay, bisexual, and transgender (LGBT) people. How the events of that night are remembered depends on who is telling the story. But one thing is certain—it was a watershed moment for the LGBT community.

NEIGHBORHOOD MAP

The Stonewall Riots took place in a five-block area of Greenwich Village, New York City. Significant landmarks are labeled on the map.

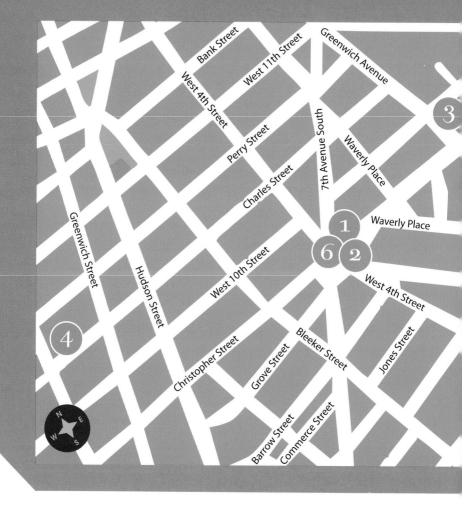

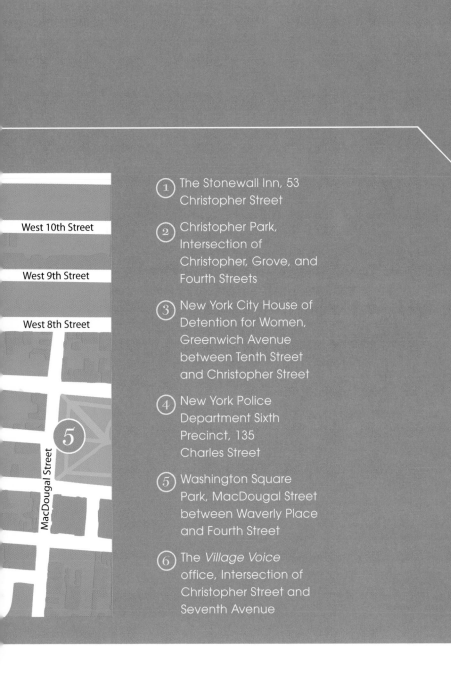

West 10th Street

West 9th Street

West 8th Street

MacDougal Street

⑤

① The Stonewall Inn, 53 Christopher Street

② Christopher Park, Intersection of Christopher, Grove, and Fourth Streets

③ New York City House of Detention for Women, Greenwich Avenue between Tenth Street and Christopher Street

④ New York Police Department Sixth Precinct, 135 Charles Street

⑤ Washington Square Park, MacDougal Street between Waverly Place and Fourth Street

⑥ The *Village Voice* office, Intersection of Christopher Street and Seventh Avenue

CHAPTER TWO
ACTIVISM BEFORE STONEWALL

Many people point to the Stonewall Riots as the spark that began the LGBT rights movement. The riots were extremely influential, but the truth is that LGBT people have always worked hard to defend themselves.

Throughout history, there are records of people who were attracted to others of the same sex, such as the Greek poet Sappho and the ancient king Alexander the Great. For thousands of years, these people were not identified with specific labels. Each culture labeled and treated them differently. They were often persecuted and considered

Alexander the Great was king of Macedonia from 336 to 323 BCE.

immoral. But for most of human history, people did not think of attraction to others as a defining identity the way society does today. Sexuality was thought of as activities a person did and not an identity a person had for life.

In the late 1800s, European scientific classification began to spread around the world. Scientific classification created a new way of thinking about the world. Everything was sorted into relationships and hierarchies. Botanists categorized plants, chemists named elements, and doctors attempted to classify human desires and attractions. A few doctors promoted the idea that same-sex attraction was innate and should not be forbidden. During the next few decades, many people who were attracted to the same sex embraced this view. They began using classifications, such as homosexual, as identities. By the early 1900s, many large cities had communities of self-identified homosexuals. However, they were still persecuted and prosecuted by mainstream society.

Because of the isolated and secret nature of many communities, early gay activism tended to be local rather than national. Without exposing their sexuality in nationwide media, it was difficult for LGBT people to coordinate a movement on a large scale. During the 1950s, however, some activists began pushing for wider recognition.

Community Disagreements

A few community organizations in the 1950s and 1960s, such as the lesbian group Daughters of Bilitis, felt it was best for LGBT people to remain quiet about their personal lives. They thought the goal of community organizations should be to help people learn to assimilate into straight culture and attain respectability.

At the time, psychiatrists categorized homosexuality as a mental illness. It was considered a moral failing that could be cured with psychiatric treatment. Although LGBT organizations disagreed with this view, in order to combat the stigma, some groups wanted to prove that LGBT people could be indistinguishable from

POLITICS OF RESPECTABILITY

Community organizations in the 1950s and 1960s were interested in cultivating LGBT respectability for many sound strategic reasons. However, organizations that focused on attaining respectability were difficult, if not impossible, for a large portion of LGBT people to work with. For gender-nonconforming people, sex workers, and homeless youth, respectability was generally not possible because it required being able to "pass" as gender-conforming and middle class. Organizational insistence on respectability directly led to fractures and exclusion within LGBT activist circles that continued for decades to come.

straight people—healthy, moral, respectable citizens. Assimilation, they believed, would eventually bring acceptance from larger society.

Other organizations, such as the Mattachine Society, disagreed with the idea of quiet assimilation. They believed LGBT people should become more visible to larger society. With greater visibility, they argued, came the ability to engage in public advocacy. Respectability was important, but largely as an effort for LGBT people to be taken seriously in their political activism. This ultimately became the approach of most well-known LGBT organizations from the 1960s going forward.

Tactics and Strategy

Gay rights activism in the 1960s was influenced in

THE MATTACHINE SOCIETY

Founded in 1950, the Mattachine Society was one of the oldest and largest gay rights organizations in the United States. The name of the group referenced an obscure French fraternal society that wore masks. Originally a radical and secretive organization run by activist Harry Hay, over the years the Mattachine Society went through drastic changes in leadership, political alignment, and strategy. By the mid-1950s, the organization was very invested in respectability as an avenue to acceptance of gay people. Over time, Mattachine Society chapters spread across the country, coordinating efforts. In 1969, the New York City chapter was firmly against any use of violence and did not support the Stonewall Riots.

HOMOSEXUALS

(ARE)

DIFFERENT...

but...

we believe they have the right to be. We believe that the civil rights and human dignity of homosexuals are as precious as those of any other citizen... we believe that the homosexual has the right to live, work and participate in a free society.

Mattachine defends the rights of homosexuals and tries to create a climate of understanding and acceptance.

WRITE OR CALL:

MATTACHINE SOCIETY INC.
OF NEW YORK

1133 Broadway, New York, N.Y. 10010   212 WA 4-7743

The Mattachine Society formed in 1950 to advocate for gay rights.

large part by the successes of the American civil rights movement. One of the major figures in that movement, Bayard Rustin, was gay. Rustin's role in the civil rights movement was generally behind the scenes, but his belief in nonviolent activism and use of tactics such as marches and sit-ins were key to the movement's strategy. These examples were inspirational for many LGBT activists.

For most LGBT activists at the time, the idea of being exposed in a public march was nearly unthinkable. But for a small, core group of activists in 1965, a public picket line seemed possible. Their strategy was to publicize the

BAYARD RUSTIN

Bayard Rustin was born in Pennsylvania in 1912. He was raised Quaker, a religion that preached equality and peace. These values, combined with his experiences of prejudice as an African-American gay man, compelled him to become an activist. Though he worked on many movements, his most influential role was as an adviser to Martin Luther King Jr. Rustin introduced King to nonviolent protest, which became the foundation of the civil rights movement. In 1963, Rustin organized the March on Washington for Jobs and Freedom, which greatly inspired leaders of the Mattachine Society. The activist strategies Rustin promoted were vital to the developing LGBT rights movement. In his later years, Rustin was active in the LGBT movement himself. He died in 1987 at the age of 75.

demands of the LGBT community by marching with picket signs in front of government buildings in both Washington, DC, and in Philadelphia. The signs bore phrases such as "Homosexuals Should Be Judged As Individuals" and "Equality for Homosexual Citizens."[1] The activists dressed conservatively, hoping to appear nonthreatening to bystanders and the press. Their actions were peaceful and quiet, so much so that they did not lead to a significant government response. Still, the picket became a yearly event called Annual Reminder Day to remind the government that LGBT people lacked the rights guaranteed in the US Constitution.

Bayard Rustin began working with Martin Luther King Jr. in the 1950s. He taught King about peaceful acts of resistance.

In 1966, a group of young activists challenged the implementation of New York State's liquor laws. State law did not explicitly prevent LGBT people from being served. However, most bars did not want them in their establishments. Some even hung signs saying, "If You're Gay, Please Go Away."[2] Inspired by lunch counter sit-ins that took place during the civil rights movement, the activists held "sip-ins" that were meant to put pressure on bar owners to serve LGBT patrons. The sip-ins were fairly successful, and in 1967, the state court finally clarified that LGBT people could be served in bars.

Out in the Streets

Before the Stonewall Riots erupted in New York, many similar riots regularly occurred in other major US cities. Although none were as infamous as Stonewall, LGBT people across the country were fighting in the streets for their rights.

In San Francisco, California, in August 1966, a riot broke out at Compton's Cafeteria, a favorite hangout of African-American and Latino transgender sex workers. For them, the café had been a safe place for many years, but a hostile new owner encouraged police to evict them. When police arrived to raid the café, harassing people and demanding to see their identification, the patrons fought back. One patron threw her coffee at an officer, inspiring others to hurl cups and dishes as the scene erupted. The raid launched a riot that lasted for two nights.

In Los Angeles, California, on New Year's Day 1967, police raided a gay bar called the Black Cat. Police threatened patrons with guns, then beat and arrested many young gay men. The following day, a local LGBT organization led hundreds of people in a protest march against the police brutality and arrests. The organization asked lawyers to witness the event in hopes of preventing further violence. Police officers watched from the sidelines but did not harass or arrest the protesters. The arrested patrons attempted to bring their case to the US Supreme Court, but they were not successful.

These and many other acts of resistance across the United States contributed to the tradition of LGBT activism in the streets. While few newspapers reported on early riots and protests, the accounts that researchers have found show how marginalized LGBT people with few resources made all the noise they could.

Building Steam

LGBT activism gained momentum throughout the 1960s all over the United States and around the world. This activism built toward the Stonewall Riots, the moment many

SEX WORK AND TRANSGENDER PEOPLE

For transgender and gender-nonconforming people, it has always been very difficult to get and keep a regular job. Many factors contribute to this situation, including societal discrimination, homelessness, and lack of family support. Historically, some transgender people, women in particular, have had to engage in sex work for survival. While it is not uncommon for transgender women to be sex workers, this fact is often exploited to perpetuate harmful stereotypes about their lives. Most transgender women are not sex workers, yet they still struggle with the stigma of the assumption that they are.

The events at the Stonewall Inn were just the beginning for the LGBT rights movement.

people consider the birth of the modern LGBT rights movement.

In some ways, it was chance that Stonewall took on a larger meaning. In other ways, it was a matter of time, place, people, and resources that shot Stonewall into history. But what exactly happened that night in Greenwich Village?

ROLE OF LGBT PUBLICATIONS

Community newsletters, magazines, and pamphlets were some of the most important tools of early LGBT activism. Organizations often published their own manifestos, as well as information on upcoming events in their cities, letters they received from subscribers, and other news. Widely circulated magazines included *ONE* and *The Ladder*, which helped spread information and opinions beyond cities with large LGBT communities. Through these print materials, activists could work around the need for mainstream newspapers, which reported very little LGBT content and rarely presented events in a sympathetic light.

CHAPTER THREE

INSIDE THE STONEWALL INN

Stuck in the back room, Raymond Castro had been waiting for what seemed like ages while the police confiscated liquor from behind the bar. They refused to answer any of his questions or even talk to any of the patrons of the Stonewall Inn. The Mafia's bar employees kept telling everyone to calm down and that everything would be all right. Castro was pretty sure they were lying. It had been 15 minutes since the raid began, and people were becoming so angry and upset it was starting to feel like a hostage situation.

Raymond Castro was a regular patron at the Stonewall Inn at the time of the riots.

The Stakes Rise

Finally, after a long wait in line and a sharp look at his identification by the police, Castro was allowed to leave the Stonewall.

He stepped into the hot, muggy air of the street, let out his breath, and walked around the growing crowd in the park, trying to decide what to do. He was not much of a political radical, but he was concerned about the people still stuck inside the bar, especially his friends. Would they be arrested? What could he do to help?

After a moment, Castro turned around and walked back toward the open door of the bar, hoping to keep an eye on the situation inside. As he reached the front of the crowd, one of his friends, still in line, caught his attention. He was gesturing frantically,

RAYMOND CASTRO

In 1969, Raymond Castro was a 27-year-old gay man who lived and worked as a baker in Brooklyn. He was a regular at the Stonewall Inn, where he felt safe dancing and holding hands with men. On the night of the raid, Castro was arrested for harassing an officer and spent the night in jail, though the charges against him were later dismissed. He helped other arrestees by paying their lawyer fees. Originally from Puerto Rico, Castro moved to Long Island several years after the riots, where he met his partner. They lived together for 30 years, until Castro died in Florida in 2010.

and Castro suddenly realized his friend did not have any identification to show the police. Without it, he would likely be arrested on suspicion of being underage. Castro looked around, hoping he could find someone to lend his friend fake identification, but before he could make a move, he was pushed.

Two police officers, angry about the growing unrest, knocked Castro down, handcuffed him, and dragged him toward the police wagon. Castro kicked and fought, but the cops threw him against the wagon's back door. Thinking fast, he planted his feet on the doorframe and pushed backward, knocking the cops down as he fell into the street. Five or six officers jumped into the fight, and in the chaos that followed, a few people escaped from the police wagon. Finally, the police threw Castro into the wagon and slammed the door shut behind him.

> "They literally carried me into the . . . wagon and threw me in there. It must've been the motivation of the crowd that inspired me to resist. Or maybe at that point enough was enough."[2]
>
> –Stonewall patron Raymond Castro

Surveying the crowd, Pine ordered the driver to deliver everyone to the jail and hurry back with reinforcements. The cops were outnumbered, and they needed backup fast.

People gathered at the Stonewall for days following the original riot.

The Standoff

As people pelted the police with coins and empty bottles, Pine knew his officers could not hold out against the crowd. A flying coin hit one of them in the face, leaving a streak of blood behind. Furious, Pine grabbed the nearest person, a tall man who he thought had thrown the coin.

Dave Van Ronk was not expecting to be involved in a riot, let alone assaulted by police. As Pine hauled him into the bar, Van Ronk fell, his head banging on the ground as he was dragged along the sidewalk. He could see the other officers grabbing more people and shoving them toward the bar. Van Ronk was sure they would all be arrested, and he was stunned by how fast everything had erupted.

Only a few minutes earlier, he had been down the street celebrating his birthday with friends. Now his hand was cuffed to a radiator, his head hurt, and a cop kept kicking him. He tried to shield himself, mind reeling. What was going on here? Why were the cops so angry?

Village Voice reporter Howard Smith came across the scene at the Stonewall Inn and ran back to his office nearby to grab his press badge. Now he had to decide whether it would be better to observe the riot from the perspective of the police or of the rioters. "You want to come in?" Pine asked him. "You're probably safer." Smith agreed.[3]

Pine yelled for his officers to get inside and lock the door. His plan was to barricade everyone inside the bar and wait for the Tactical Patrol Force (TPF) to arrive. The cops pushed tables and large pieces of wood against the door. The front window was always covered in plywood so curious passersby could not see inside the bar. Afraid it

DAVE VAN RONK

Folk singer Dave Van Ronk was a well-known fixture in the coffee shops of Greenwich Village. He was straight and not part of the LGBT community, but on the night of the raid, he happened to be near the Stonewall Inn. He had been at another bar down the block when he heard shouting in the street. Curious, he went outside and made his way into the crowd at the door of the Stonewall Inn. He was arrested for throwing coins at police officers.

Dave Van Ronk was a folk singer who was well known in the 1960s Greenwich Village music scene.

would not hold up against the angry crowd, the police quickly reinforced it with two-by-fours.

As the crowd outside began to heave things at the door, Smith could see the cops were frightened. They had been arrogant, and this time it backfired. Pine tried to keep order by assigning each of his officers to a post: the back room, the window, and the hall. Guns drawn, the police threatened to fire at any intruders, while the patrons inside waited nervously for what was to come. Smith, scared for his own safety, found a big wrench behind the bar and tucked it in his belt.

The floor shuddered and the door buckled, swinging open. A volley of bottles and trash flew inside the bar before the cops forced the door shut again. Again and again, the rioters and the police battled at the door. One of the officers shouted, "Get away from there or I'll shoot!"[4] Then the covered window buckled and

THE *VILLAGE VOICE*

Though at the time the *Village Voice* was not known for being pro-LGBT, it was one of the few news outlets to report on the Stonewall Riots in any depth. The Greenwich Village–based alternative newsweekly was founded in 1955 and prided itself on a different kind of reporting. Articles were often written using contemporary slang and with an interest in nonmainstream issues and politics. This style of reporting eventually spread across the nation, and alternative newsweeklies became a staple of city life.

the glass shattered. A bottle flew through the opening and hit a wall inside the bar. Filled with gasoline, the bottle exploded into a small fire on the floor. Another bottle followed.

The cops grabbed the fire hose and extinguisher, rushing to put out the blazes. Then they aimed the hose out the window, hoping to blast it at the rioters, but only a trickle of water came out. The floors became slippery inside the bar. Tension was sky-high, and all of the cops were checking their guns in case they needed to fire.

The patrons and employees inside the bar, still held captive by the police, did not know what to do. Pine questioned one of them fiercely, a Mafia employee who knew all the escape routes in the building. Then Pine sent an officer, a small woman, to shinny through a vent in the ceiling. Pine told her to run to a pay phone and call the police station

TACTICAL PATROL FORCE

In the 1960s, the New York Police Department's Tactical Patrol Force was an elite unit of riot police officers. Required to be large, strong men, the officers were trained to subdue crowds using nightsticks, shields, and tear gas. They wore helmets with plastic visors and used huge plastic shields to form human walls that were impossible to break through. The TPF was feared and hated by many people in New York because of its history of violence against marginalized communities.

to find out where the riot squad was. None of their radio communications were going through.

The roar of the crowd outside the bar terrified Smith. It sounded like a real riot, like fighters determined to avenge their friends and take back what was theirs. A trash can full of burning paper crashed into the coatroom. Someone outside threw lighter fluid and a burning match through the window. Pine aimed his gun at the shadowy figure. Then suddenly, the wail of sirens cut through the night.

CHAPTER FOUR

OUTSIDE THE STONEWALL INN

Stormé DeLarverie had just gotten off work
when she stopped by the Stonewall Inn. It was
approximately 1:30 a.m., but as an entertainer,
DeLarverie worked unusual hours. She had
been uptown all night, emceeing a drag show
at the famous Apollo Theater in Harlem. Still
dressed in men's clothes, DeLarverie was
easily mistaken for a gay man, but she was a
butch lesbian who spent her nights performing
as a drag king.

The Stonewall Inn was one of DeLarverie's
regular stops after work. She saw herself as a
security guard for the LGBT community, and
she liked to make rounds to check in with bar
patrons. By the time she got to Christopher

Stonewall Inn patrons tried to keep police
from conducting their raid.

Street, however, she could see something dangerous was brewing. A crowd was gathered in the small park across from the Stonewall Inn. Police were milling around outside the door.

DeLarverie pushed through the crowd until she could see what was going on. A young man lay injured on the ground by the entrance. Worried for him and used to protecting people, DeLarverie did not hesitate. She rushed to his side and attempted to help him stand up, but a police officer grabbed her roughly by the shoulder and yelled at her to move along.

DeLarverie refused to leave the injured man, explaining to the officer that she was only trying to help. The officer shouted at her again, raised his nightstick, and hit her across the face. The nightstick smacked and

Stormé DeLarverie was one of the most prominent figures of the gay rights movement.

stung, but DeLarverie remained unafraid. Having faced prejudice and abuse all her life, she knew exactly how to deal with a bully. DeLarverie drew back her fist and punched the cop hard.

The Riot Fires Up

The crowd erupted. As the cops began pushing arrested patrons into the back of the police wagon, loud boos filled the air. Seeing their friends harassed and assaulted yet still fighting back empowered others in the crowd. People circled the wagon, pushing and rocking it back and forth as if to bust it open and liberate the people within. Shouts echoed with accusations of police brutality and demands for freedom. Empty cans and copper pennies flew at the arresting officers, striking their ducking heads and clanging into the street. In just a few moments, the patrons of the Stonewall Inn all agreed they were done with taking insults and indignities.

In the midst of the crowd, Marsha P. Johnson was furious. She had been out celebrating and was not in the mood to deal with police harassment. Most days, she was an easy target for the vice squad, who were always looking to arrest people for cross-dressing. Johnson could hardly count the number of times she had been booked before, both for the way she dressed and for how she made her living as a hustler. She had come to the Stonewall Inn to relax with her friends, not to fight with the police. Still, if the cops brought the fight to Johnson's doorstep, she was not going to back down. She had been living on the street for years, and she knew very well how to fight dirty. When she saw officers assaulting patrons, she grabbed a cobblestone from the ground, heaved it at the police, and screamed, "You can't do that!"[2]

As the police retreated into the bar, the bottles and cans the crowd threw turned to bricks and cobblestones.

> "I'm sick of being told I'm sick."[3]
>
> -Rioter Kevin Dunn

The rioters and the cops battled over the door. They yelled threats at each other as the crowd bashed the door open and the cops dragged it closed again. Two muscular gay men wrestled with a damaged parking meter, trying to pry it out of the cracked sidewalk. It had been hit by a car and was bent at an angle, and the men rocked it back and forth until they managed to uproot it. Holding the parking meter like a battering ram, they slammed it repeatedly into the door of the bar. *Boom. Boom.* Each time, they backed up across the street and then ran at the door full tilt while the crowd cheered and threw rocks.

MARSHA P. JOHNSON

Marsha P. Johnson came to Greenwich Village from New Jersey in the early 1960s. Well-known in her community of transgender hustlers and LGBT street youth, she was kind and generous with any resources she had. She told people her middle initial stood for "Pay it no mind," a phrase she used to dismiss rude questions about her gender.[4] Johnson spent many years living on the street and was committed to looking after younger hustlers, particularly transgender women. With Sylvia Rivera and other activists, she founded a communal living and advocacy organization. Johnson's style was infamous; she reused found items to create accessories, such as flower crowns and hair jewelry. In 1975, she posed for a portrait series by gay pop artist Andy Warhol. She died in 1992 at age 46, found in the Hudson River. Though friends suspected she was murdered, her death was ruled a suicide and never investigated by police.

Marsha P. Johnson was a well-known gay rights activist.

For 45 minutes, the patrons outside the bar fought to take back the Stonewall Inn from the police who had barricaded themselves inside. The

> "We wanted . . . to go after the police and free the Stonewall."[5]
>
> –Rioter Michael Fader

siege went on and on. A few people began setting fire to bits of paper and stuffing them in the crack under the boarded-up window in order to smoke out the police. It was not successful. The sparks did not last long enough to create much smoke, and the rioters had to quickly dash away from the window in case the police decided to shoot.

Then someone in the crowd had the idea to create makeshift Molotov cocktails—empty beer bottles filled with gasoline that would explode into small fires when they hit the bar floor. If the bar caught fire, the police would have to abandon the building and rush headfirst into the crowd. No one had a real plan for what would happen then, but everyone wanted to get back at the cops for harassing them, and makeshift tools were all they had.

Several bottles crashed into the wall of the bar, flames jumping free. The crowd grew larger and angrier. They were going to take back what was theirs. Within an hour and a half of the raid's start, the patrons outside the Stonewall Inn had the police cornered.

The Riot Squad Shows Up

The sirens were the first sign that the situation was about to change. Two large fire trucks had been circling the riot, trying to find a way through the crowded streets. Finally, they forced their way in, pulling up outside the bar along with several local Sixth Precinct police cars. Their red lights whirled across the scene as they radioed for the TPF to send a riot squad. In another moment, the police wagon returned, ready for more prisoners. Very quickly, the mood of the situation shifted. The police were embarrassed that LGBT people had bested them, and they were angry enough to do almost anything in revenge.

Soon, two buses full of riot police spilled out onto Christopher Street. Similar to soldiers, they formed unbroken lines for combat. The crowd of rioters scattered but soon regrouped. Swinging their nightsticks, the TPF officers advanced on the crowd, moving in a tight V-shaped wedge. The crowd broke up again under the force of the violence, retreating as the riot police pushed forward. But a few groups of rioters ran right around the block, coming up behind the officers to regroup once more. They yelled chants and threw bottles at the back of the police formation, preventing the officers from clearing the streets and beginning a back-and-forth confrontation.

WE ARE THE STONEWALL GIRLS

One of the most infamous stories from the Stonewall Riots showcases the humor and defiance of LGBT street youth. Weeks earlier, several young gay men had made up a jokey song about the Village girls. It was sung to the tune of "Ta-Ra-Ra-Boom-De-Ay." They would perform it while walking down the street with their arms linked, kicking like a chorus line. It tended to frighten straight people, which made the street youth laugh. During the riot, the group changed the lyrics and sang the song while dancing in a kick line. The TPF stared in shock at the spectacle. The new lyrics were:

We are the Stonewall girls

We wear our hair in curls

We wear no underwear

We show our pubic hair[6]

The crowd's resistance was fierce and determined, even as they were beaten and chased. They taunted the police, surrounding them from both sides of the street. Then they hurried down hidden alleys to catch up to the police when they moved. The street youths' knowledge of the Village's quirky layout allowed them to slip away from the riot squad many times. Around and around the crowd went, groups peeling off every block, leading the police one way and then chasing them another. To many in the crowd, the riot felt almost like a dream—there was no sense of time, only the ongoing rush of actions and movement. Years of resentment and humiliation at the hands of the police channeled into the adrenaline of a street battle the LGBT community felt like they could win. There was a sense of communal purpose and excitement that the revolution had finally come.

> "I'd been waiting for this to happen. . . . I had tears of joy. And I was willing to do anything."[7]
>
> –Rioter Jerry Hoose

The TPF had weapons that the rioters did not have, however. They turned large hoses on the crowd and beat anyone in their path, from rioters to curious bystanders. Still, the TPF could not control the riot. Eventually, in the early hours of Saturday morning, the crowd began thinning out of its own accord. After fighting with the TPF and running through the streets all night, groups began splitting off from the crowd. They drifted away to catch up with friends and recount their experiences. By four o'clock in the morning, the full moon hung over streets that were eerily quiet.

ARREST RECORDS

During the raid on the Stonewall Inn, the New York Police Department arrested several patrons. The arrest reports explain the crimes they were charged with.

COMPLAINT REPORT

Complainant:
Wolfgang Podolski

Date and time:
3:00 a.m.,
June 28, 1969

Place:
53 Christopher St.

Type of Premises:
Club

Crime
Felony Assault

Details: Defendant did strike arresting officer with a rolled up newspaper, causing officer to fall to ground.

COMPLAINT REPORT

Complainant:
Marilyn Fowler, Raymond Castro, and Vincent Depaul

Date and time:
2:00 a.m., June 28, 1969

Place:
53 Christopher St.

Type of Premises:
Club

Crime
Harassment

Details: Defendants did shove and kick the officer.

COMPLAINT REPORT

Complainant:
Dave Van Ronk

Date and time:
2:00 a.m., June 28, 1969

Place:
53 Christopher St.

Type of Premises:
Club

Crime
Felony Assault

Details: Defendant did throw an unknown object, which struck the officer in the right eye causing injury.

CHAPTER FIVE

SATURDAY NIGHT

The next day, Saturday, was the hottest June 28 ever recorded in New York City. It was hotter than Friday had been and miserably humid. But even so, groups of LGBT people gathered on Christopher Street outside the Stonewall Inn. Word of the riot spread up and down the city during the day, and by the time it was dark outside, the police had taken notice of the growing crowd. They kept the groups moving, trying to disrupt any protests before they could start. But by midnight, the crowd had swelled to thousands and the chants had started to pick up. "Liberate Christopher Street," someone yelled.[1]

A sign chalked outside the Stonewall Inn in early July 1969 asked locals to stop demonstrating.

Out in the Open

People in the crowd held hands, kissed each other, and told campy jokes at the top of their lungs. Being LGBT out on the streets was a new experience for most of them. The idea that they could make noise about who they were and who they loved was astonishing to them. There was no hiding and no shame, in part because they were surrounded by other LGBT people like themselves. It was an utterly transformative moment in many of the protesters' lives.

The crowd was not made up of only LGBT people, though. Many straight people had come, whether to watch the spectacle or to join in out of support for the cause. One straight woman lectured a police officer: "Don't you know that these people have no place to go, and need places like that bar?"[2] Another straight woman, however, inched through the crowd in horror, muttering to herself that the gathering must be some evil product of the full moon. The crowd was so huge that five blocks of Greenwich Village around the Stonewall Inn were essentially closed off.

"It was an absolutely exhilarating experience. . . . All of a sudden we were out on the streets. We were there. . . . And it was incredible."[3]

–Rioter Chris Babick

Inspired by the chants about liberating the street, a group of protesters decided to make it a reality. Standing shoulder to shoulder, hundreds of people blockaded Christopher Street. Traffic ground to a halt. With arms linked, the group declared this was now a gay street and no straight people were allowed to pass through. Mirroring the way police required identification before LGBT people were allowed to leave raided bars, any people who wanted to come through the blockade had to prove their identity. The protesters wanted to show straight people how it felt to be singled out and harassed.

Round Two Begins

As more police cars arrived on the scene, the protest began shifting into another riot. The crowd targeted the

CAMP HUMOR

A historically gay sense of humor and style, camp is a complex concept. In terms of humor, it usually refers to a witty and theatrical way of joking. Campy jokes often use double meanings or have multiple layers of humor. They are told in a self-aware, knowing manner, and are often meant to highlight the absurd or unexpected. Using humor that relied on being in the know was one way gay people could identify each other and reinforce a sense of community and belonging. Camp could be a way to tease insiders as well as a way to mock outsiders. In the case of the Stonewall Riots, LGBT street youth used the campiness of their gender nonconformity to outwit and frustrate the TPF's violence.

Sylvia Rivera was a key figure in the civil rights and gay rights movements of the 1970s.

reinforcements, throwing bottles at their cars. Sylvia Rivera, a friend of Marsha P. Johnson, hurled rocks and yelled at the police. Down the block, an abandoned construction site provided an ample supply of bricks. Johnson, who had returned after the first night of rioting, gathered up a pile of discarded bricks and stuffed them into her bag. She had used this method before, as many hustlers did, to create a makeshift weapon in case a sexual encounter went bad and the man became violent.

This time, Johnson clutched the bag, hiked her legs up around a streetlight, and began to shimmy her way up the pole. People watched from below, amazed. When she reached the top of the pole, Johnson let the bag of bricks drop onto a police car's windshield. The satisfying smash of thick glass seemed to propel the riot forward, as a symbol of the cops' authority and freedom from consequences had been explosively destroyed.

Other rioters began tossing anything they could find at police cars. One cop got a face full of wet, stinking coffee grounds when a garbage bag burst

SYLVIA RIVERA

A lifelong activist for LGBT people, particularly transgender women, Sylvia Rivera was known as a force to be reckoned with. Rivera was born in New York City. Her mother was Venezuelan and her father was Puerto Rican. Her mother died when she was three, and Rivera began hustling and living on the street at age ten. She survived by banding together with other LGBT street youth and was later mentored by Marsha P. Johnson. By the time Rivera reached her late teens, she was very concerned about the welfare of younger hustlers. With her friends, she founded a communal house and advocacy group to help take care of transgender street youth. Rivera was a tough and determined activist who forced others to pay attention to the most marginalized members of the LGBT community, even when they preferred not to. She died in 2002 at the age of 50.

all over his window. Another had a concrete block dropped on the hood of his squad car. The crowd cheered and clambered onto the hood and up to the car's roof, pounding and dancing on top of it before moving on. The next cop car's red flashing light was ripped off and thrown away. Rioters shook the empty vehicle back and forth, pushing so hard it seemed it might tip over.

Officers grabbed anyone who got near their cars, arresting people almost at random. The massive crowd was utterly out of their control. Police attempts to interrupt the street blockade continued without much success until just after two o'clock in the morning, when the TPF was called in. As the squads met to discuss strategy, a skirmish erupted.

Two police officers broke off from the group and, at random, pulled a young gay man out of the crowd. They dragged him to the police wagon and held him down while four more officers beat him with nightsticks, assaulting his face, stomach, and crotch. Someone in the crowd screamed for help, and suddenly a mass of fem gay men descended on the officers, rescued their friend, and spirited him back into the safety of the crowd. The officers chased after the group but were confronted by a chain of rescuers, arms linked, who did not abandon their posts when the cops began beating them.

The bravery of gender-nonconforming LGBT people is one of the most remarkable aspects of the Stonewall Riots. They were on the front lines of the fighting, perhaps because they were more likely to be targeted by police for their manner and style. Often, they used their nonconformity to disrupt and frighten police, cleverly countering the cops' harassment with outrageous guerilla tactics. The police did not know how to handle such unexpected actions. One participant remembers it was the gender-nonconforming rioters' "sense of humor and 'camp' that helped keep the crowds from

GENERATIONAL AND CLASS DIVIDES

Older, middle-class gay men were among those who came to the Stonewall Inn on Saturday night to see what was going on. They had heard of the previous night's riot and were cautiously hopeful about the reports of LGBT resistance, but most of them were not pleased by what they found. They disapproved of the violent protests, and few of them identified with the younger gender-nonconforming people on the street. As one man said, they were "limp-wristed, shabby, or gaudy gays" who straight-passing gay men were afraid to associate with.[5] This respectability divide was an enduring issue in LGBT politics for years to come.

WHERE WERE THE BUTCH MEN?

With a few notable exceptions, gender-conforming gay men were generally not on the front lines of the Stonewall Riots. In fact, one bystander saw a message to them chalked on the sidewalk: "Butches, where are you now that we need you?"[7] From numerous accounts, butch or gender-conforming gay men were involved in the riots, but the most visible LGBT rioters were the fem or gender-nonconforming people who fought back furiously.

getting nasty."[6] Though the riots ultimately did get fairly nasty, the rioters themselves understood the absurdity of the scene and capitalized on it.

Still, the TPF returned for a second night, and the situation again became violent. The squad assembled in a flying wedge formation, as they had the night before. Marching up the street, they resembled a solid wall, their massive plastic shields bulldozing anyone in their way. Sweeping rioters out of their way, the TPF emptied Christopher Street, putting an end to the gay blockade. But some rioters still resisted the police, singing and dancing as they had before. Their kick line faced off with the advancing TPF until the squad was almost upon them. Then, the rioters turned and scrambled down side streets, repeating tactics from the previous night, popping up behind the TPF to taunt and yell.

The riot police continued to be brutally violent, handling their nightsticks like swords, cracking bystanders over the head and beating rioters bloody. Within half an hour, the streets were under their control, though it took another hour before the last rioters dispersed. For two hours that night, Christopher Street had belonged to the LGBT crowd, and although they could not keep it, a seed had been planted in their minds.

CHAPTER SIX

THE NEXT NIGHTS

Sunday morning dawned on empty streets outside the Stonewall Inn. Most of Saturday night's rioters were sleeping, but one of them was making plans. Craig Rodwell did not sleep at all that night. He stayed up, feverishly writing a manifesto titled, "Get the Mafia and the Cops out of Gay Bars." Printed as a one-page flyer, his manifesto called on LGBT people to boycott Mafia-run bars and demand a stop to the police corruption that allowed the Mafia to corner that market. Rodwell believed LGBT people should be able to run their own bars without fear.

Later in the day, as people gathered on Christopher Street, Rodwell's activist friends

Craig Rodwell advocated for gay rights for more than 30 years. He owned the Oscar Wilde Memorial Book Shop in Greenwich Village.

distributed thousands of the flyers. There was a sense among those who had rioted that the events of the past few days could be a turning point, as long as they did not lose momentum. Many people had spent the weekend talking with their friends, wondering what might happen next and how activists could feed the spark of the Stonewall Riots.

Other LGBT activist organizations, however, thought differently. The Mattachine Society decided to cooperate with the police in order to defuse the political tension. On Sunday afternoon, a sign appeared in the window of the Stonewall Inn: "We homosexuals plead with our people to please help maintain peaceful and quiet conduct on the streets of the Village—Mattachine."[1] Despite the group's established place in the community, its plea went largely unheeded by younger, more radical activists who dismissed Mattachine as old fashioned.

What Happens Next?

The mood on Sunday night was one of tense watchfulness. No one was quite sure what to expect, but people showed up outside the Stonewall Inn anyway. No one wanted to miss a moment of the astonishing events. Still, the crowd was smaller than it had been on previous nights, and for the first time there were more cops than protesters on the streets. Ironically, in an attempt to restore order,

The Mattachine Society hung a sign in the window of the Stonewall Inn asking rioters to act peacefully.

police officers were actually begging groups of LGBT people to go inside the Stonewall Inn. The Mafia had cleaned up the bar and served free nonalcoholic drinks, trying to charm patrons back. Members of the Mattachine Society joined the effort, hoping to prevent further rioting. It was a strange alliance, to say the least.

Even though the streets were much quieter, there were still acts of defiance and opposition to the police presence. The crowd of LGBT people outside the Stonewall Inn continued to circulate political flyers and pamphlets, recount their experiences of the previous nights, and discuss what they should do next. They did not hide their sexuality, and they took up public space without apology. One group of protesters even took advantage of the fact that there were very few officers remaining back at the Sixth Precinct headquarters. Sneaking up to the police station, they plastered bumper stickers on the cars in the parking lot. In bright neon colors, the stickers proclaimed, "Equality for Homosexuals."[3]

The TPF had already been summoned to the bar for the night and were standing by, waiting for violence to erupt, but there was very little for them to do. Around one o'clock in the morning, as the crowd began to disperse, the riot squad made a sweep of the blocks around Christopher Street. As the squad assembled in formation, poet Allen Ginsberg happened to walk down the street. Being a gay man, Ginsberg had decided to check out the scene after hearing about the riots. Upon seeing the riot squad, he flashed a peace sign and strolled into the Stonewall Inn. Ginsberg had not been to the bar before and was amazed at how confidently the gay men inside carried themselves. Years ago, he had stopped going to gay bars because he disliked the pervasive sense of shame and self-hatred there. It was astonishing to witness this new sense of pride and purpose. It seemed to Ginsberg that change was finally coming.

Allen Ginsberg was a poet and one of the best-known beatniks.

A Brief Intermission

Monday and Tuesday nights were even quieter than Sunday
night. Many people felt the need for rioting was over now
that LGBT people had proven they were willing to stand
up for themselves. What more could be gained at this
point? Other people were busy organizing new activist
groups, energized and radicalized by the weekend's
events. And almost everyone had other places to be and
other work to do. For the most part, the protesters who
remained outside the Stonewall Inn were LGBT street
youth, hustlers, and a few other activists who wanted to
keep an eye on the police presence.

The activists' instinct that something more was
to come turned out to be a good one. The police

were still feeling the sting of embarrassment at being outmaneuvered by a group of people they considered morally and physically weaker. Many of the male police officers felt their masculinity had been challenged along with their authority. Some of those officers were angry enough to pick fights with the smaller crowd, taunting and insulting them until they snapped.

The protesters who remained at the Stonewall Inn were just as angry as the cops, and just as willing to engage in conflict. One cop harassed every gay man who walked by until one of them turned around and taunted him back. The man was arrested on the spot. Another cop who threatened passersby had a firecracker thrown at him, and yet another got involved in a scuffle and had his badge stolen. Though the scale of these clashes was much smaller, the streets were still not entirely settled.

"The big thing on everyone's mind . . . was that these were the only rioters that had gotten the best of the police. So that gave them a special strangeness. . . . *How could that happen?*"[4]

–Riot witness Bob Kohler

The Fire Reignites

On Wednesday, an entirely new outrage spread like wildfire through the LGBT community. Two of the reporters who had witnessed the Stonewall Riots published their accounts on the front page of the *Village Voice*. Their reporting was condescending toward LGBT people, and one article in particular was full of mean-spirited and insulting comments. In the past, the newspaper had been dismissive toward LGBT people, and community activists disliked its editorial policy, believing it to be hypocritical. A crowd gathered outside the newspaper offices. Some of the people were so angered they discussed setting fire to the building, but no one took the initiative to do so.

By Wednesday night, news of the riots had reached many straight radical activist groups, and they showed up in force. Some of them were curious to learn more about what had happened, and they wanted to establish solidarity with the rioters.

Other activist groups, however, were primarily interested in taking advantage of the unstable situation to protest for their own causes. By ten o'clock in the evening, a huge crowd had assembled on Christopher Street. People lit fires in trash cans, chanted slogans, and threw bottles at patrolling police cars. The mood was grim and angry, entirely lacking the campy humor of the weekend riots.

> "Everybody sensed that nothing was going to be the same after this. We just knew."[5]
>
> –Rioter Craig Rodwell

The local police and the TPF were angry too, and it showed in their tactics. They did not hesitate to wield their nightsticks or their fists, beating rioters bloody and dragging them down the street to the police wagons. Very quickly, the scene became incredibly violent, and the straight activists fled, along with many LGBT activists. Within one hour, the Stonewall Riots were over. The neighborhood cleared of everyone but the locals, and in the aftermath, Christopher Street resembled an abandoned battlefield. Injured people lay in the street, bruised and bleeding. Many of them were the same LGBT people who had fought for days to liberate that space for themselves.

CHAPTER SEVEN

THE IMMEDIATE IMPACT

For LGBT people living in Greenwich Village, the Stonewall Riots were life changing. Many of them had participated, of course, but even among those who had not protested, there was a profound change in attitude. Their community had succeeded and bested the police. This accomplishment encouraged a new sense of confidence and hope for the future. It was a heady feat for a largely unorganized crowd, most of whom did not consider themselves political activists. But for those who did, and those who simply felt they had been waiting their whole lives for the revolution, this moment was not to be wasted.

Annual Reminder Day took place each year on July 4 at Independence Hall in Philadelphia.

Cracks in the Foundation

Only a few days after the Stonewall Riots, there was a peaceful protest in Philadelphia organized by several older LGBT activist organizations, including the Mattachine Society. The protest was known as Annual Reminder Day and had occurred on July 4 for four years. But this year, many younger participants thought it felt like a throwback, an outdated and conservative way of representing the LGBT community. Protesters had to wear gender-conforming clothing, quietly march single file, and behave as respectably as they would in church.

After the revelation of the Stonewall Riots, Annual Reminder Day felt repressive and pointless

ANNUAL REMINDER DAY

Begun in 1965 by the Mattachine Society, Annual Reminder Day was a public protest bringing awareness to the lack of LGBT civil rights. Activists picketed in front of Philadelphia government buildings, carrying signs bearing demands and slogans. The original 1965 protest was one of the first times in US history a group of LGBT people marched openly in public. Organizers Frank Kameny and Barbara Gittings are often called the father and mother of the modern LGBT rights movement, though they were not involved in the Stonewall Riots. The last Annual Reminder Day protest was in 1969.

to many activists who attended the event. One young lesbian couple decided to push the envelope just slightly by marching next to each other holding hands. To the older activists, this was a counterproductive act of disobedience. They broke up the couple and chastised them furiously. It was a moment that brought into sharp focus the massive gap growing between generations of LGBT activists. For young activists, it was clear they needed to organize their own groups if they wanted to protest in a more radical way.

At a public Mattachine Society meeting in New York City that same night, screaming matches erupted about how the group should respond to the Stonewall Riots. The Mattachine activists called for a measured response: a peaceful vigil that would not draw violence from the police. They explained that maintaining respectability would lead to acceptance from authority. Others in the crowd found that approach infuriating. They were tired of being told to tone down their anger and hide their expressions of gender nonconformity. It seemed clear a serious break in LGBT political leadership was coming.

"We have got to radicalize. . . . Be proud of what you are. . . . All the oppressed have got to unite!"[2]

–Gay Liberation Front activist Jim Fouratt

Growing Pains

Despite the obvious shift toward radical politics in the younger generation of LGBT activists, there was still the question of how to unite under one banner. The first attempt to do so was a march against police harassment on the one-month anniversary of the Stonewall Riots. On July 30, 500 people gathered around the fountain at Washington Square Park near New York University. Their plan was to march to the small park outside the Stonewall Inn and to the Sixth Precinct police station, carrying signs and chanting. The banner they created for the march was lavender-colored, and people wore armbands made of the same fabric. Speakers called on the crowd to get organized and stand up for themselves so there would never be another "reign of terror" like the one police maintained over LGBT people.[3]

The march was a success in that it convinced many onlookers that gay power might be a legitimate movement rather than a flash in the pan. The marchers halted traffic, gaining attention and confidence as they progressed toward the site of the riots. The tradition of memorializing the Stonewall Inn as a landmark for gay rights began at this march. Internally, however, march organizers were in conflict about whether they should target the Sixth Precinct police station. In the end, the crowd did not march on to confront police, and this change in plan led to further fractures in activist leadership circles.

At a meeting the next day, the radical activists involved in the march voted to establish an organization called the Gay Liberation Front (GLF). This group, they believed, would be more effective and forward-thinking because its activism would not focus solely on gay rights. The GLF would fight for the rights of all oppressed groups. It would even fight to end the war in Vietnam (1954–1975). The GLF believed solidarity was the answer, and its manifesto proclaimed: "a common struggle . . . will bring common triumph."[4] While in line with radical politics of the era, the manifesto was drastically different from the targeted focus of established gay rights groups, such as the Mattachine Society.

GAY LIBERATION FRONT

The Gay Liberation Front (GLF) was founded one month after the Stonewall Riots occurred. Originally formed as a committee to plan the July 1969 march against police harassment, the group solidified and grew into an organization. It was the first LGBT group to openly claim gay identity in its name. Over the years, the GLF held many more marches and protests, ran radical study groups, and fund raised for various causes. Eventually, due to diverging political interests, the organization split into several smaller groups, known as cells, each with their own focus and objectives.

The GLF quickly found a foothold with young LGBT radicals, but its path was a difficult one. The group decided it would not have any leaders despite its growing size. Its goal was to avoid the problems that came with hierarchy and to create a space where everyone's ideas were valued equally. In practice, however, this became chaotic and unfair. People in the majority opinion tended to talk over dissenting voices. The organization struggled internally, but GLF's magazine, *Come Out!*, and events the group organized were extremely popular with young activists.

The Gay Liberation Front (GLF) marched at Times Square in New York City in 1969.

The GLF regularly hosted fund raising dances as an alternative to Mafia-run gay bars. For many attendees, the dances were like paradise—no harassment, no overcharging, and no straight people. But most of the lesbians in the GLF felt excluded by the way the dances mimicked the atmosphere of gay men's clubs. After some discussion, they decided to create separate dances for women. When Sylvia Rivera and Marsha P. Johnson started Street Transvestite Action Revolutionaries (STAR), the GLF also held dances to fund raise for the group.

Several members of the GLF were disillusioned

STAR IS BORN

Sylvia Rivera and Marsha P. Johnson founded Street Transvestite Action Revolutionaries (STAR) in 1970. The two activists and several of their friends were concerned about the welfare of younger hustlers, particularly transgender women, and wanted to create a communal home. At first, they lived in an abandoned trailer, and later they rented a burned-out building from the Mafia in exchange for fixing it up. Young household members did not have to hustle for a living. Instead, older members, including Rivera and Johnson, contributed their earnings and food to the group. The STAR house was a safe space for transgender street youth, but within a year, the Mafia evicted the group, and they never found another home. STAR continued on as an activist organization until 1973. After a public confrontation with transphobic lesbians at Christopher Street Liberation Day, Rivera was devastated, and STAR faded out.

Rivera attended a protest with STAR outside New York City's Bellevue Hospital, which practiced shock therapy on gay psychiatric patients.

with the way the organization supported issues other than gay rights. It frustrated them that sometimes, instead of using money raised at dances to fund an LGBT initiative, the members voted instead to donate it in solidarity to the Black Panther Party or the Young Lords, a Puerto Rican group. The GLF believed that supporting other radical activist groups built trust and common ground, but not everyone agreed. After many discussions, a small group split off from the larger organization, wrote up its own manifesto, and named itself the Gay Activists Alliance (GAA). Somewhat more conservative in focus and tone, the organization nevertheless aggressively challenged political figures to support gay rights.

Around the same time as this break came a serious test of the unity of the LGBT activist community. Rodwell and a few of his friends proposed a memorial march on the one-year anniversary of the Stonewall Riots. Scheduled for June 28, 1970, the event would require a massive amount of planning and coordination. Whether the community could pull it off was a very real question.

GAY ACTIVISTS ALLIANCE

The Gay Activists Alliance was founded in December 1969 as a splinter group from the GLF. The GAA was the first LGBT group to use the Greek letter lambda as a logo, which is now associated with many LGBT organizations. While the GAA was less politically radical than other organizations, it was incredibly influential in terms of strategy. The group developed an activist tactic it called zaps, which used a sudden, shocking public action to gain media attention for an issue. The GAA's first zap involved shouting gay slogans at an opera performance attended by the mayor. The highly effective tactic was key for later generations of LGBT activists.

CHAPTER EIGHT
THE STONEWALL LEGACY

At first, not many New York LGBT organizations were terribly interested in commemorating the one-year anniversary of the Stonewall Riots—or at least not in Rodwell's vision. He and three friends proposed changing the Mattachine Society's Annual Reminder Day into a nationwide event called Christopher Street Liberation Day. Although their proposal was accepted by the East Coast chapters of the Mattachine Society, Rodwell had difficulty convincing local groups to join in and help organize. Even the leader of the New York City chapter of Mattachine

The first Christopher Street Liberation Day Parade started at the Stonewall Inn. People marched up Fifth Avenue to Central Park.

declared himself against the idea. It seemed the LGBT movement was so ideologically divided that cooperation was not possible.

An Uphill Battle

The planning committee for Christopher Street Liberation Day was made up of just eight people. Most of them were members of the GLF and Mattachine Society, but they were not overwhelmed by support from their organizations. The group struggled to raise the $1,000 needed to put on the event, pleading for donations from anyone they could think of. Twenty dollars of their budget was actually found by chance on a sidewalk in Greenwich Village. Organizers cut the budget as much as they could. They reduced the planned two-day event to a simple protest march. They found a graphic designer who was willing to donate his time to make flyers, and then they photocopied the flyers for free at their day jobs.

By the time June 28 rolled around, Rodwell was not sure how many people would show up to march. The day was sunny and cool, a good sign, and in the past few weeks the GAA had stepped up its involvement, putting up flyers all over the Village. But there were problems getting the necessary permits from the police to hold the event. Although the permits came through at the last minute, the organizers had no real way of knowing whether the people who assembled at the beginning of the march route would stick it out until the end. No one was sure how the group would be received on the streets, and many people were afraid of attacks. The planning process was so fraught it seemed impossible the event could go off without incident.

Police set up sawhorses to block traffic and stood

> "I decided I would march, but I left little clauses in my mind. If I didn't feel good, I wouldn't go. If there was any violence, I would drop out."[1]
>
> –Crowd marshal for Christopher Street Liberation Day

around looking bored, sometimes cracking jokes at the expense of the gathering crowd. The numbers were low at first, just a few hundred people. Marching together, they would take up only one city block. By the time the march was due to start, many in the crowd were obviously nervous. Half of them hung back near the curb, unsure whether they would actually march or simply see the group off. The organizers waited, hoping for a larger crowd to arrive and reassure people of their safety.

Finally, under pressure from the police and unable to wait any longer, the organizers ordered everyone into formation. Some 20 organizations assembled, marching under their own banners and carrying signs. At the front of the crowd, Rivera stood confidently, more used to public scrutiny and dealing with the police than most of the other protesters. As the crowd moved forward, Rivera led chants.

"What do we want?" she yelled.

"Gay power!" answered the crowd.

"When do we want it?"

"Now!"[2]

Reclaiming the Streets

At first, everyone marched briskly, unsure how bystanders would react to the group. But as blocks passed and no violence broke out, people began to relax. Little by little, as it became clear no one was targeting the group, LGBT onlookers joined the march from the sidewalks. The crowd grew, just as the organizers hoped.

By the time the march reached Twenty-Second Street, one-third of the way along the planned route, the crowd was 15 blocks long. No one could believe it, least of all the organizers. And still, the most common reaction they received was simply stunned silence as they passed. Tourists snapped

"It was clear to me from then on. . . . I had to save and protect myself by committing to my own liberation. It was like work time."[3]

–Marcher and activist
Yvonne Flowers

photos in amazement, people in stopped cars stuck their heads out their windows to stare, and shocked passersby froze in their tracks. None of them had ever seen such a huge crowd of LGBT people, let alone a crowd carrying signs saying, "I am your worst fear, I am your best fantasy," and chanting the words, "Out of the closets and into the streets!"[4]

In the last leg of the march, on a hill in Central Park, many marchers paused to look back at the crowd behind them. It trailed seemingly forever, on and on through the streets of Manhattan. No one could see where it ended.

Gay Pride

In 1970, a few other US cities took up Rodwell's proposal to hold an anniversary march for the Stonewall Riots. Los Angeles was the most prominent participant, but Chicago and other places held demonstrations as well. Afterward, news

THE MARCH IN LOS ANGELES

With 1,200 participants, the 1970 Christopher Street Liberation Day march in Los Angeles was the second-largest in the country.[5] A local chapter of the GLF had helped organize the event, which represented 30 different organizations in the area. A more outspoken and daringly dressed group than the New York crowd, the marchers also dealt with more heckling and harassment from onlookers. Undaunted, the activists carried banners, signs, and huge props that one participant described as "so Hollywood."[6]

The Christopher Street Liberation Day Parade became an annual event.

spread of how well many of the marches turned out. By the next year, marches were organized in even more cities, including several in Europe.

Over the next few years, the celebration of LGBT resistance became a worldwide event. Brenda Howard, one of the original organizers, was in large part responsible for this success through her continuing work on the march. Howard was also instrumental in renaming the event Gay Pride, a phrase that seemed to encompass the larger spirit of the project. The concept of gay pride was influenced by African-American pride slogans from the civil rights movement. For example, Frank Kameny adapted "black is beautiful" into "gay is good."[7] An LGBT group in Los Angeles called Personal Rights in Defense

DYKE MARCHES AND TRANS MARCHES

In 1993, members of the activist group Lesbian Avengers began to organize women-led marches that coincided with Gay Pride. These informal events, affectionately called Dyke Marches, were meant to provide a space during Gay Pride for women to gather and share community. More politically oriented than contemporary Gay Pride, Dyke Marches continue in the spirit of protests rather than parades. Begun in San Francisco in 2004, Trans Marches are similarly political. Organized to protest high rates of murders of transgender people and to raise awareness about transgender issues to Gay Pride, Trans Marches spread quickly to many other cities.

For the twenty-fifth anniversary of the Stonewall Riots, gay rights activists carried a one-mile- (1.6 km) long rainbow banner along New York City's First Avenue to Central Park.

and Education (PRIDE) may also have contributed to the rise of gay pride.

With an annual international event promoting LGBT causes, activism and awareness increased dramatically. Gay Pride quickly became a community rallying point for most activists. But organizationally, significant differences in political alignment, focus, and tactics still remained. No single event could eliminate the internal arguments of a marginalized community or resolve the long-standing frictions between groups. Regardless, one of the legacies of the Stonewall Riots is certainly the surge of energy that created Gay Pride, which continues to prompt activism today.

LGBT Activism

The other major legacy of the Stonewall Riots is the rise of radical politics in LGBT activist circles, leading to a fundamental shift in how such organizations function. The change in viewpoint and strategy that occurred between groups, such as the Mattachine Society and the GLF or GAA, fed directly into the ways later generations of activists understood and undertook their work. For example, in the 1980s, AIDS Coalition to Unleash Power (ACT UP) used direct action to aggressively attract attention to their cause. The proliferation of activist groups during the 1970s continued onward, bearing new alliances, ideas, and struggles.

In the decades since the Stonewall Riots, there have been many victories for LGBT rights. In 1973, after intense lobbying by activists, the American Psychiatric Association removed homosexuality from its list of mental illnesses. In 1980, following the National March on Washington for Lesbian and Gay Rights, the Democratic Party became the first major US political party to endorse an LGBT rights platform. In 2003, after years of activists filing constitutional challenges, the US Supreme Court ruled that state laws banning same-sex sexual activity were

On June 27, 2016, the Stonewall Inn was designated as a national monument.

unconstitutional. These and many more hard-fought battles, such as marriage equality, have been won, and even more continue.

Keeping the Spark Alive

In 2016, President Barack Obama announced the creation of the Stonewall National Monument as a National Park Service site. The increased attention and funding will help preserve the historic site of the Stonewall Riots for generations to come. The place where LGBT people stood

MARRIAGE EQUALITY

In 2015, the US Supreme Court ruled that state laws banning same-sex marriage were unconstitutional. After many years of piecemeal legislation and court cases, same-sex marriage became legal across the entire United States. The legislative history of marriage activism spanned more than 20 years, including many steps forward and then back again. The issue of marriage was always contentious within the LGBT community, but the legal rights and protections that went along with it were considered extremely important.

up to police harassment and built the groundwork for future activists is one of the most evocative sites in LGBT history. Through communal memory, it has become almost mythical in proportion, but its reality is more humble. It was a place where hustlers and street youth let down their guards, where a dirty floor was nothing to complain about, and where the people who rioted were the ones who had the least to lose. Honoring and telling their stories every year at Gay Pride marches is one way to keep the spirit of the Stonewall Riots going strong.

In 2011, Phyllis Siegel (arms raised) and Connie Kopelov became the first same-sex couple to get legally married in New York City.

TIMELINE

1800s

Doctors attempt to classify human desires and attraction.

LATE 1800s

European doctors publish studies asserting that same-sex attraction could be innate.

EARLY 1900s

Communities begin identifying themselves as gay.

1912

Bayard Rustin is born.

1950

Harry Hay founds the Mattachine Society, an early gay rights organization in the United States.

1950s

Greenwich Village becomes a common beatnik community; some gay rights organizations begin pushing for better recognition.

1960s

New York laws state people must wear at least three articles of gender-conforming clothing in order to avoid arrest; the American civil rights movement influences the gay rights movement.

1965

The Mattachine Society begins Annual Reminder Day, using public picketing to bring awareness to gay rights.

1966

Activists associated with the Mattachine Society engage in "sip-ins" to challenge New York State liquor laws regarding LGBT bar patrons; San Francisco Police raid LGBT hangout Compton's Cafeteria, setting off riots.

1967

As a result of the sip-in actions, New York State clarifies that it is legal to serve LGBT bar patrons; Los Angeles police raid LGBT bar the Black Cat, prompting a public protest march.

JUNE 28, 1969

An early-morning police raid on the Stonewall Inn, a LGBT bar in New York City, sets off five nights of riots and protests.

JULY 1969

LGBT activists found the Gay Liberation Front (GLF) one month after the Stonewall Riots.

JULY 30, 1969

LGBT activists hold a march one month after the Stonewall Riots to protest police harassment.

DECEMBER 1969

LGBT activists found the Gay Activists Alliance (GAA).

1970

Sylvia Rivera and Marsha P. Johnson found Street Transvestite Action Revolutionaries (STAR).

JUNE 28, 1970

LGBT activists hold the first Gay Pride event, Christopher Street Liberation Day, a march to commemorate the one-year anniversary of the Stonewall Riots.

1973

The American Psychiatric Association removes homosexuality from the list of mental illnesses.

1980

The Democratic Party becomes the first major US political party to endorse an LGBT rights platform.

1993

The first Dyke Marches take place.

2002

The Transgender Law Center and Sylvia Rivera Law Project form to help tackle legal issues faced by the transgender community.

2003

The US Supreme Court rules state laws banning same-sex sexual activity are unconstitutional.

2004

The first Trans Marches take place.

2015

The US Supreme Court rules state laws banning same-sex marriage are unconstitutional.

2016

President Barack Obama designates the Stonewall National Monument at the site of the Stonewall Riots.

ESSENTIAL FACTS

KEY FIGURES

- Seymour Pine was the NYPD deputy inspector who led the police raid on the Stonewall Inn.

- Raymond Castro, a gay patron, was arrested for fighting police at the Stonewall Inn.

- Dave Van Ronk, a straight bystander, was arrested at the Stonewall Inn for harassing police.

- Stormé DeLarverie, a lesbian, was assaulted by police at the Stonewall Inn and fought back.

- Marsha P. Johnson was a transgender patron who rioted at the Stonewall Inn.

- Sylvia Rivera was a transgender patron who rioted at the Stonewall Inn.

- Craig Rodwell was a gay patron who rioted at the Stonewall Inn and later proposed the first Gay Pride march.

KEY STATISTICS

- Approximately 200 patrons were at the Stonewall Inn on the night of the police raid.

- More than 1,000 people participated in the Stonewall Riots.

- Approximately 2,000 people participated in New York City's first Gay Pride march.

IMPACT ON SOCIETY

The Stonewall Riots of June 1969 inspired the first Gay Pride march, held in June 1970. Gay Pride eventually became an annual event in cities around the world, spreading awareness of and activism for LGBT rights and issues.

QUOTES

"The best metaphors for Stonewall are words like *home*, because when you're not living anywhere regularly, home becomes what you make it."

–Stonewall patron and gay street youth Tommy Lanigan-Schmidt

GLOSSARY

ASSIMILATE
Blend in; resemble or liken.

BISEXUAL
A person who is attracted to others of the same gender and of a different gender.

BOHEMIAN
A person, often a writer or artist, with an unconventional or wandering lifestyle.

BUTCH
An LGBT person whose gender identity or expression leans towards masculinity.

CONFISCATE
To take away or seize someone's property.

DRAG KING
A female performer who dresses as a man for the purpose of entertaining others at bars, clubs, or other events.

DRAG QUEEN
A male performer who dresses as a woman for the purpose of entertaining others at bars, clubs, or other events.

FEM
An LGBT person whose gender identity or expression leans toward femininity.

GENDER-NONCONFORMING
A person whose gender expression is different from societal expectations related to gender.

HUSTLE
To earn money by engaging in sexual activities with others.

LGBT
The acronym for lesbian, gay, bisexual, and transgender.

PASS
To be considered a member of an identity group different than a person's own.

RADICAL
Supporting political reform by changing social structures and values.

SEX WORKER
A person who earns money by engaging in sexual activities with others.

TRANSGENDER
A person whose gender identity, expression, or behavior is different from those typically associated with their assigned sex at birth.

TRANSVESTITE
An outdated, now offensive term for a person who dresses in clothing traditionally or stereotypically worn by a different sex.

VICE SQUAD
A police unit that deals with crimes involving things seen as personal vices, such as gambling, pornography, prostitution, and illegal drugs.

ADDITIONAL
RESOURCES

SELECTED BIBLIOGRAPHY

Carter, David. *Stonewall: The Riots That Sparked the Gay Revolution.* New York: St. Martin's, 2004. Print.

Cohen, Stephan L. *The Gay Liberation Youth Movement in New York: "An Army of Lovers Cannot Fail."* New York: Routledge, 2008. Print.

Faderman, Lillian. *The Gay Revolution: The Story of the Struggle.* New York: Simon, 2015. Print.

FURTHER READINGS

Bausum, Ann. *Stonewall: Breaking out in the Fight for Gay Rights.* New York: Viking, 2015. Print.

Pelleschi, Andrea. *Transgender Rights and Issues.* Minneapolis, MN: Abdo, 2015. Print.

Watson, Stephanie. *Gay Rights Movement.* Minneapolis, MN: Abdo, 2013. Print.

WEBSITES

To learn more about Hidden Heroes, visit **booklinks.abdopublishing.com**. These links are routinely monitored and updated to provide the most current information available.

FOR MORE INFORMATION

For more information on this subject, contact or visit the following organizations:

GLBT HISTORY MUSEUM
4127 Eighteenth Street
San Francisco, CA 94114
415-621-1107
http://www.glbthistory.org/museum/
The GLBT History Museum features exhibits on LGBT life from the 1940s to today.

ONE NATIONAL GAY & LESBIAN ARCHIVES
909 West Adams Boulevard
Los Angeles, CA 90007
213-821-2771
http://one.usc.edu/
ONE National Gay & Lesbian Archives is the largest collection of LGBT materials in the world.

STONEWALL NATIONAL MONUMENT
Intersection of Christopher, Grove, and Fourth Streets
New York, NY 10014
212-668-2577
http://www.nps.gov/ston/
The Stonewall National Monument is a developing National Park Service site.

SOURCE NOTES

CHAPTER 1. THE RIOT

1. David Carter. *Stonewall: The Riots That Sparked the Gay Revolution.* New York: Saint Martin's, 2004. Print. 86.

2. Ibid. 142.

3. Ibid. 150–152.

CHAPTER 2. ACTIVISM BEFORE STONEWALL

1. Lillian Faderman. *The Gay Revolution: The Story of the Struggle.* New York: Simon, 2015. Print. 152.

2. Ibid. 117–119.

3. Ibid. 143.

CHAPTER 3. INSIDE THE STONEWALL INN

1. "Complete Program Transcript: Stonewall Uprising." *American Experience.* PBS, n.d. Web. 18 Sept. 2016.

2. Marcus Franklin. "Stonewall Rebel Reflects 40 Years after NYC Riots." *OutHistory.org.* Associated Press, 27 June 2009. Web. 29 May 2016.

3. David Carter. *Stonewall: The Riots That Sparked the Gay Revolution.* New York: Saint Martin's, 2004. Print. 157.

4. "Stonewall at 40: The *Voice* Articles That Sparked a Final Night of Rioting." *Village Voice.* Village Voice, 24 June 2009. Web. 29 May 2016.

CHAPTER 4. OUTSIDE THE STONEWALL INN

1. William Yardley. "Storme DeLarverie, Early Leader in the Gay Rights Movement, Dies at 93." *New York Times*. New York Times, 29 May 2014. Web. 29 May 2016.

2. David Carter. *Stonewall: The Riots That Sparked the Gay Revolution*. New York: Saint Martin's, 2004. Print. 298.

3. Ibid. 161.

4. Ibid. 65–66.

5. Ibid. 166.

6. Ibid. 176.

7. Ibid. 179.

CHAPTER 5. SATURDAY NIGHT

1. David Carter. *Stonewall: The Riots That Sparked the Gay Revolution*. New York: Saint Martin's, 2004. Print. 182–183.

2. Ibid. 184–185.

3. Ibid.

4. Martin Duberman. *Stonewall*. New York: Dutton, 1993. Print. 203.

5. David Carter. *Stonewall: The Riots That Sparked the Gay Revolution*. New York: Saint Martin's, 2004. Print. 187–188.

6. Ibid. 192.

7. Ibid. 184–185.

SOURCE NOTES
CONTINUED

CHAPTER 6. THE NEXT NIGHTS

1. David Carter. *Stonewall: The Riots That Sparked the Gay Revolution.* New York: Saint Martin's, 2004. Print. 191–195.

2. Lillian Faderman. *The Gay Revolution: The Story of the Struggle.* New York: Simon, 2015. Print. 184.

3. David Carter. *Stonewall: The Riots That Sparked the Gay Revolution.* New York: Saint Martin's, 2004. Print. 197–199.

4. Ibid. 202.

5. Ibid. 196.

CHAPTER 7. THE IMMEDIATE IMPACT

1. Edmund White. "Letter to Ann and Alfred Corn." *OutHistory.org.* Center for Lesbian and Gay Studies at the City University of New York, June 2009. Web. 29 May 2016.

2. Martin Duberman. *Stonewall.* New York: Dutton, 1993. Print. 211.

3. David Carter. *Stonewall: The Riots That Sparked the Gay Revolution.* New York: Saint Martin's, 2004. Print. 218.

4. Lillian Faderman. *The Gay Revolution: The Story of the Struggle.* New York: Simon, 2015. Print. 196–197.

CHAPTER 8. THE STONEWALL LEGACY

1. Martin Duberman. *Stonewall*. New York: Dutton, 1993. Print. 275.

2. Ibid. 277–278.

3. Ibid. 279.

4. Harry Gu. "Revolutionary Love." *InVisible Culture: An Electronic Journal for Visual Culture*. InVisible Culture, 5 Feb. 2014. Web. 19 Sept. 2016.

5. Martin Duberman. *Stonewall*. New York: Dutton, 1993. Print. 278–279.

6. Ibid.

7. "Frank Kameny." *LGBT History Month*. LGBT History Month, 2016. Web. 14 Aug. 2016.

INDEX

ABOUT THE
AUTHOR

Tristan Poehlmann is a freelance writer of educational nonfiction on history, science, and art. A former museum exhibit developer, he has worked on exhibits about LGBT history, Mary Shelley's *Frankenstein,* and famous inventors. He holds a master's degree in writing for children and young adults from Vermont College of Fine Arts. He lives in the San Francisco Bay Area.